*Kissing the Dancer & Other Poems*

# KISSING THE DANCER
# & OTHER POEMS

*By Robert Sward*

INTRODUCTION BY WILLIAM MEREDITH

*Cornell University Press*  ITHACA, NEW YORK

© 1964 by Cornell University

CORNELL UNIVERSITY PRESS

*First published 1964*

*Second printing 1964*

Library of Congress Catalog Card Number: 63-23368

PRINTED IN THE UNITED STATES OF AMERICA

*For Diane*

# INTRODUCTION

These poems are unusual and excellent in a number of ways, but what strikes me first about them is that they are the only book of poems I know about – well, maybe one of two I know about – that has been turned down by a lot of publishers over a good many years because they are so original as to be unrecognizable as poetry by a conventional eye. They have gone off to respectable publishers with praise from Stanley Kunitz, Louise Bogan, even Robert Lowell, and come back with the embarrassed confession that they simply escaped the respectable editors. I submit that this is very rare today, when so many books of poems are printed every month and the squarest publishers are looking for poetry with the dogged altruism of philanthropists.

Randall Jarrell recently described a school of prosperous, mild-talented poets as seeming to have come out of the lining of Richard Wilbur's overcoat. The poets of another school, who appear to get into print pretty easily, strike me as having their home at the bottom of William Carlos Williams' laundry hamper. You cannot recognize Robert Sward's poems by any such affinity. They come out of original experience and they exist in language that the experience discovered. And if that is the least that can be said of any book of real poems, it means more when a book presents experience as odd as this one does. I was tempted to the impertinence of this introduction because I was curious to see if I could say why these poems have delighted and puzzled me for six years.

From reading Robert Frost I have learned to look for giveaway lines in poems, hidden lines that tell the sly reader some of the secrets by which a poet works. "The bird would cease and be as other birds / But that he knows in singing not to sing," in "The Oven Bird" are two such lines. With Sward these secret lines are not only hidden but often apparently in the negative, recounting apparent creative errors. "My examples are all myself," he says, implying that that's wrong. But the poem "For Charlie," where the line occurs, shows that in fact it's right: that once you get a good fierce look at the example of self — the only example any of us will ever have — you can see the world in it. I think Sward believes that.

And he writes (in "All for a Day"):

> All day I have written words;
> My subject has been that. Words.
> And I am wrong. And the words.

But there are a hundred lines in this book which seem to have found their sweet, eccentric selves in this very pre-occupation. Certain entire poems like "In Cities" (and perhaps "All for a Day" itself) take life from a fierce intensity of verbal attention.

And here is a stanza that can probably be taken at its face value as poetics, although I'm not saying it will make the problem of writing poems a whole lot easier for any of us:

> I am fond of death — and/or
> The self-contained. This poem may not be said to be
> About souls. But of things. Feathers and leaves.
> Leafless trees and the featherless bodies of crows.
> Finally, let us say, I have been asked to write simply.

As nearly as we can ever know these things about one another, I know that Robert Sward works long and hard on his poems. I have asked myself, What does he work on about them? I mean, they don't rhyme or scan, like some of my glossy works, and they don't allude to American History. I have come to the conclusion that when he works on them he is paying perfect, slightly mystical attention to the things he's tipped us off to above: (1) himself as an example of a man; (2) his vocabulary as a butterfly net to catch the experiences the man has; and (3) a passion for simplicity. His simplicity is not that of Zen (now there's a gamy laundry hamper to breed poets in) or of Thoreau, but something more like that of Blake or Emily Dickinson. If you look at things long enough with this kind of attention they sometimes resolve themselves into pure creation: you find yourself using italics, *and they're not yours — they're created italics.* Here is a section of a poem called "Scenes from a Text," which has the fairly hair-raising epigraph "'Several *actual*, potentially and/or really traumatic situations are depicted on these pages.' — *Transient Personality Reactions to Acute or Special Stress* (Chapter 5)."

PHOTO II
The house is burning. The furniture
Is scattered on the lawn (tables, chairs
TV, refrigerator). Momma —
There is a small, superimposed white
Arrow pointing at her — is busy
Tearing out her eyes. The mute husband
(Named, arrowed) stands idly by, his hands
Upon his hips, eyes already out.
*The smoke blankets the sky.* And the scene,
Apart from Momma, Poppa, the flames . . .
Could be an auction. Friends, relatives
Neighbors, all stand by, reaching, fighting
For the mirrors, TV, sunglasses;
The children, the cats and speechless dogs.

Like other good works of art, these poems have the air of having been made for people rather than for other artists. They contain high-toned gossip rather than aesthetics, or the aesthetics are hidden and acted out like charades. A lot of the poems are unpleasant in places, like life itself, but none of them contains any fashionable despair. No claim is advanced that our time is more terrible or hopeless than another or, on the other hand, that you and I don't have experience as the poet has experience. There is that humility about them that comes from paying a blasphemous attention, God's own attention, to oneself. I myself couldn't work that way, and I couldn't have written this book, but I think I will soon be in good company when I say I much admire it.

WILLIAM MEREDITH

# ACKNOWLEDGMENTS

Grateful acknowledgment for permission to reprint is here given to the following magazines, chapbooks, and anthologies:

*Ambit* (London), for "Letter to His First Dog"; *Antioch Review*, for "Before Firing" and "The Ceiling"; *Approach*, for "By the Swimming"; *Arts in Society*, for "Snow"; *Beloit Poetry Journal*, for "The Apteryx (1/35) of Webster's Dictionary and New Zealand"; *Carleton Miscellany*, for "My Students," "*Saturday Review* – Classified; Personal," and "Voyage"; *Chelsea Review*, for "All the Mornings," "Classified – Pets," "Dedication," "Emu: A Lecture for Voices; for Stereo," "Photos of Some Poets," and "There Is No Reason Why Not to Look at Death"; *Chicago Review* and *Chicago Review Anthology*, for "Uncle Dog: The Poet at 9"; *Contact*, for "For Charlie."

*Epoch*, for " '. . . I Have Just Bought a House' "; *Galley Sail Review*, for "Socrates at the Symposium"; *Hudson Review*, for "Attic by the River" and "Elm Trees"; *Mt. Shasta Selections*, for "Dodo" and "Scenes from a Text"; *The Nation*, for "Mothers-in-Law," "Owl," "The Weather," and "What It Was"; *New Orleans Poetry Journal*, for "In Cities" (formerly entitled "Underground") and "The Kite"; *Odyssey Chapbook Number One (Advertisements)*, for " 'The Very Air He Breathes.' "

*Paris Review*, for "All for a Day" and "Nightgown, Wife's Gown"; *Poetry*, for "Barbecue," "An End to Doubt," "Kissing the Dancer," "A Letter to His Psychiatrist," "Lost Umbrellas," "Marriage," "Miss Elderli Dora Des Moines – One March," "Pet Shop," "Steeple," "Terminal Theater," "Turnpike," and "A Walk in the Scenery"; *Poetry Northwest*, for "The Cyclades"; *Quarterly Review of*

*Literature,* for *"National Geographic"*; *Riverside Poetry III* (Twayne Publishers, Inc.), for "The Kite"; *Satis* (England), for "The Immortals, in Question"; *Shenandoah,* for "For Stones."

"That That All Encloses," © 1963 by the Chrysalis West Foundation, is reprinted from *Genesis West* by permission of the publisher.

Some of the poems in this volume also appeared in *Uncle Dog and Other Poems* (London, 1962), and are here reprinted with the kind permission of the publisher, Putnam & Co., Ltd.

Finally, I wish to thank the Corporation of Yaddo and the Edward MacDowell Association for affording me an opportunity to complete this book.

R. S.

# CONTENTS

*Kissing the Dancer & Other Poems*

# UNCLE DOG: THE POET AT 9

I did not want to be old Mr.
Garbage man, but uncle dog
Who rode sitting beside him.

Uncle dog had always looked
To me to be truck-strong
Wise-eyed, a cur-like Ford

Of a dog. I did not want
To be Mr. Garbage man because
All he had was cans to do.

Uncle dog sat there me-beside-him
Emptying nothing. Barely even
Looking from garbage side to side:

Like rich people in the backseats
Of chauffeur-cars, only shaggy
In an unwagging tall-scrawny way.

Uncle dog belonged any just where
He sat, but old Mr. Garbage man
Had to stop at everysingle can. ˙

I thought. I did not want to be Mr.
Everybody calls them that first.
A dog is said, Dog! Or by name.

I would rather be called Rover
Than Mr. And sit like a tough
Smart mongrel beside a garbage man.

Uncle dog always went to places
Unconcerned, without no hurry.
Independent like some leashless

Toot. Honorable among scavenger
Can-picking dogs. And with a bitch
At every other can. And meat:

His for the barking. Oh, I wanted
To be uncle dog — sharp, high fox-
Eared, cur-Ford truck-faced

With his pick of the bones.
A doing, truckman's dog
And not a simple child-dog

Nor friend to man, but an uncle
Traveling, and to himself —
And a bitch at every second can.

# THE KITE

I still heard Auntie Blue
After she did not want to come down
Again: she was skypaper, way up
Too high to pull down. The wind
Liked her a lot, and she was lots of noise
And sky on the end of the string:
And the string jumped hard all of a sudden,
And the sky never even breathed,
But was like it always was, slow and close
Far-away blue, like poor dead Uncle Blue.

Auntie Blue was gone, and I could not
Think of her face; and the string fell down
Slowly for a long time. I was afraid to pull it
Down. Auntie Blue was in the sky,
Just like God. It was not my birthday
Anymore: and everybody knew, and dug
A hole, and put a stone on it
Next to Uncle Blue's stone, and he died
Before I was even born; and it was too bad
It was so hard to pull her down; and flowers.

# WHAT IT WAS

What it was, was this: the stars
Had died for the night,
             and shone;
And God, God also shone,
Up, straight up, at the very
Top of the sky.
             The street
Was one of the better suburbs
Of the night, and was a leaf,
Or the color of one in the
Moonlit dark.
             She, my mother,
Went to the window; it was
As late as night could be
To her.
             She looked at the wind,
Still, the wind,
             . . . never having blown.

And in the morning, now, of sleep
The stars, the moon and God
             began
Once more, away,
             into the sky.
— And she, my mother, slept . . .
In her window, in her sky.

# A WALK IN THE SCENERY

It is there. And we are there. In it.
Walking in it, talking, holding hands.
The nickel postcard — the glossy trees;
The waterfalls, the unsuspecting
Deer. A scene shot from a car window:
A slowly moving car, with many
Windows, and a good camera.
And we are walking in it. We tell
Ourselves, quietly, perhaps screaming,
. . . Quietly, *We are walking in it.*
And our voices sound, somehow, as if
We were behind windows, or within.
We embrace, and are in love. The deer
That we are watching, at the same time
(Through cameras, binoculars, eyes . . . )
Are so perfectly wild, and concerned
— With the scene they are, their glossy fate
Silence, Nature, their rotogravure pose —
That they remain, not watching; rather,
Staring away from us, into the
Earnest, green and inoffensive trees.

# MARRIAGE

I lie down in darkness beside her,
This earth in a wedding gown;
                Who, *what*
She is, I do not know.
Nor is it a question the Night
Would ask. I have listened —
                The woman
Beside me breathes. I kiss that,
A breath or so of her, and glow.
                Glow.
Hush now, my shadow, let us
*Day breaks* —
                depart.
Yes, and so we have.

# LOST UMBRELLAS

She enters a room exuding displeasure,
    strewing bits of string, grievances
        bottlecaps
        hairnets
   law books
   like largess
To all corners.

From the seams of her changepurse
      leak
      Travelers Cheques,
Photos of used-car salesmen
     (dear brothers-in-law),
  strychnine,
    ragged old horoscopes
And gifts of broken glass.

Daughter to the planet Saturn,
Mother to my wife —

Her courtiers, we direct her,
Mix martinis for her
Find causes for her, lost umbrellas
    and carkeys
Even at the gates of hell.

# IN CITIES

There are many underground things
in cities, things like sewers,
that run for miles, lengths
and widths, across cities,
under all. Then there are
the basements of large stores,
houses and hotels, and often
these basements run for twenty feet
and more out, around the buildings;
and coal, garbage and all kinds
of food are sent up and down into
the basements, or out, from the sidewalks and the alleys and streets,
by chutes, corrugated elevator-
stands, iron platforms, sewertops
. . . round, rectangular or square.

And these metal things in the sidewalks,
streets, are always rather warm;
and in the winter, to comfort
and unbitter their sittings,
haunches and tails, and to avoid
the asphalt ice and cold, cats
and dogs, stray squirrels
and so forth, come at night
and from miles around, rest
and together partake.
                    And from some
distances, they and their live optic
green, brown congregations of eyes
appear as islands, still yellow
large, oval, gray or opalesque.

8

And no dog bites no cat, nor squirrel,
and all is quiet, idle, until the sun
comes up and chases them
out of the night, off the warmth
and good of the sewers to their parts
and tails. Then without a look
at the sun, itself, they run, trot
walking, no, no business into the snow.

# NATIONAL GEOGRAPHIC

## SCENES FROM A SUPPLEMENT ISSUE

I

### THE WAI-WAI INDIANS

*British Guiana, thirty-seven*
*Hundred pygmy aborigines,*
*A group shot.* Faces, the New England
Autumnal, Kipling-Kodachrome shade
Of nipples. They gape and seem about
To drop: like leaves.
                    Stare. Faces. The faces
Stare. And breathe, breathe.

                        Their breasts (the tribe
Is composed wholly of women) stand
Out like twigs, gnarled, like rotten, thick
Knotted bra-wire. Monkey-teeth are embedded
In the tips and glisten, they glisten
In the white, eye-dot "flash," like jewels;
*In the flash, in what makes the flash . . .*
Faces. The faces are intent, still,
And gape. They are leaves, miraculous,
Savage, maple leaves. Sentient. Like coal,
Like death, like both; like leaves.
                      The faces
Grin for an instant, grin and then fall,
In an instant
             — thirty-seven hundred leaves.

## II

THE AUTHORS EAT AS WAI-WAI DO

Spitted, twelve hundred Yaka-Yaka villagers,
Men, women and children, constitute
The evening meal. ("The Yaka-Yaka,
Pygmy-pygmies, are as chicken
                    to the Wai-Wai.")
The author and his wife, Mrs. Flash,
In Yaka-Yaka moccasins, share
A leg, while the thirty-seven hundred Wai-Wai
Pass among themselves ribs, entrails . . .
With fingers (and toes) for the chief.

WAI-WAI DINNER SONG

*Queen's Monkey-teeth:*

> Eat, we eat, little people;
> Mmm. Eat, eat little people.
> Fingers, toes; eyes and hair;
> Good to eat and bones to wear.
>
> Eat, we eat, little people;
> Mmm. Eat, eat little people.
> Neck and brains, sugared tongues;
> Good to eat, as good as lungs.

*Mrs. F.'s Flash Bulbs:*

> Eat, we eat, little people;
> Mmm. Eat, eat little people.
> Juicy, tender, pygmy boys;
> Mothers, fathers, spitted toys.
>
> Eat, we eat, little people;
> Mmm. Eat, eat little people.
> Eat their mouths, eat their faces;
> Eat their skin, eat the traces.

*Chorus:*
> Yaka-Yaka, Yaka-Yaka;
> Yaka-Yaka, Yaka-Yaka.

## III

PHYSICAL MEASUREMENT TEST

The little Wai-Wai chieftain,
"Forty-one pounds, three-foot nine,"
Stands upon a bathroom scale,
A nude, encircled silhouette
In the great, white island moon.
Her monkey-tooth gleams, as if
It were the moon, behind her,
Within her, shining through her.
And she stands there, a small, black
*National Geographic*
Anthropological queen . . .
Still. She stares. "A leaf-like face;
A driftwood piece of trunk,
With limbs, twigs — "
           upon the scale,
In the embracing, fluorescent
Newly BRILLIANT! inched, notched
Calibrated moon. She sways . . .

## IV

TYPHOON THREATENS EXPEDITION: A SEQUENCE

*The moon goes out, melts and is absorbed*
*Into the air;*
       *becomes a heat, Night,*
*Coolness, a humid stillness,*
          *a breeze . . .*

It breaks, gray —
            the wind becomes a gale;
Palm trees, coconut fronds, pink parakeets,
Splash across the sand. Yaka-Yaka,
Wai-Wai, Mr. and Mrs. Flash. *Teeth.*
Night, the night opens, and is darker
Than before,
            Night, the night lightnings, black
And is a sea, falling from the sky.
Calm. The authors bind together trees,
Buoyant Wai-Wai, coconuts,
                        flash bulbs;
Life preservers, parakeet feathers . . .
The sprightly, befeathered raft sets out,
Mr. and Mrs., Yaka-Yaka;
Leica, new bulbs and film;
Wai-Wai breasts and leaves,
Vaguely fluorescent, bubbly, still. Stone.
It sinks. Like stone, stone
                        into the sea.
      *       *       *

Wai-Wai, thirty-six hundred
Ninety Wai-Wai,
            huddle together,
Shuddering, glancing at, nibbling
*National Geographic*
            leaves, leaves
The photos, the faces of themselves.

## THE APTERYX (1/35) OF WEBSTER'S DICTIONARY AND NEW ZEALAND

The inflected apteryx (or kiwi) would appear
To be a rudimentary, an essentially
Webster-bird. The apteryx (from the Greek *a* +
*Pteryx*) does not fly and, in fact,
Lacks all regard (and need) for flight.

Flat-breastboned, hen-sized and scratchy,
The apteryx stands on two declining
And unlikely chicken-legs. It *ooou*'s for food
Through a long, thin reed-like beak:
Insects, snails, crippled fleas and berries.

The nostrils of the apteryx
Are at the last half-inch of its beak.
And the bird — not quite extinct — survives
Under government protection. It reproduces
Slowly, and in public, burrow-hiding.

If its hairs were feathers, ocellated
Aphrodisiacal, the sleepy, marginal, asterisk-eyed
Apteryx could (conceivably) strut, cock
And play the peacock; however, with its one hint
Of a tail, and grayish, short shag-brown hair

The apteryx would seem content to *ooou*. And,
Its beak alone, apt and straight, endears it
To one; but when it curls itself, extinct
Within its sleeping back (by day),
Enwhiskering its *ooou*, the apteryx returns
Upon the government and Webster of it all.

# OWL

Let us suppose the truth:
I am an owl by virtue
Of my belief in owls.

The owl swoops, like a hawk;
Is still, like a rock; shrieks,
Meditates, like God,
                    like air.

I believe in owls. And,
What is more, what is in fact
The exact same thing, as you
Will by now have guessed,
                          I am

Hawk, rock, rodent, wail
                    and God.
Which troubles me, which makes
Of me, myself. An owl.

# KISSING THE DANCER

*For Diane, who dances*

Song is not singing,
    the snow

Dance is dancing,
    my love

On my knees, with voice
    I kiss her knees

And dance; my words are song,
    for her

I dance; I give up my words,
    learn wings instead

We fly like trees
    when they fly

To the moon, which
    on occasion

They do; there, there are
    some now

The clouds opening, as you, as we
    are there

        Come in!

I love you, kiss your knees
    with words,

Enter you, your eyes
    your lips, like

Lover
Of us all,

words sweet words,
learn wings instead.

## ELM TREES

Down hill, the elm trees
In the sunlight,
Their trunks darkish
Under branches, under leaves.
Higher up the hill
In this woman's arms
I see through to the other side
As into another season,
The sun suddenly all
On one side of the leaves.

# BY THE SWIMMING

By the swimming
The sand was wetter
The farther down you dug; I dug:
My head and ear on top
Of the sand, my hand felt water  . . .
And the lake was blue not watching.
The water was just waiting there
In the sand, like a private lake.
And no one could kick sand
Into my digging, and the water
Kept going through my fingers slow
Like the sand, and the sand was water too.
And then the wind was blowing everyplace,
And the sand smelled like the lake,
Only wetter. It was raining then:
Everybody was making waxpaper noises,
And sandwiches, kicking sand
And running with newspapers on their heads;
Baldmen and bathinghat-ladies, and nakedpeople.
And all the sand turned brown and stuck together
Hard: and the sky was lightning, and the sun
Looked down sometimes to see how dark it was
And to make sure the moon wasn't there.
And then we were running: and everybody was under
The hotdog-tent eating things, spitting very mad
And waiting for the sky, and to go home.

# MERT

Mert was a moron . . . plainly
decently, kindly, honestly
and with his whole heart,
Mert was a moron, and a good one.

Mert did just what he did,
often forgot, it's true
but did
as long as he did
and remembered
to do.

Mert smiled
without a thought,
without a muscle
dumbed down in his face;

Mert laughed
with his entire tongue,
entire throat, and every one
of his teeth:
and with his hands
as happy as a million hundred seals.

Mert did in a minute!
more than a fox
more than a bear
more than a maybe (-r);

Mert met a girl, a mother
kind of girl.
And the girl said, Mert —
and Mert said, Yeah?

19

and the girl said
and said and said and said

And Mert smiled
without a muscle, without
a thought; and went away
with a
with a
with a
without a did
without a do.

# TERMINAL THEATER

We fight. I am clubbed from behind. They pin me
And take turns, forearm feet fists to face
Forefinger and thumb opening eyelids, press
Graze with the nail, touch with the palps
Squash, the Jew's eyes seeing eye, sand
Sprinkle, candlewax, cigarette ash,
Cigar smoke. It is necessary to see this
Against a backdrop of __
For four miles west of it one can smell
The lake; further, it being July, the water
Tastes of chlorine stale fish breath snail-dew
Sharks

Even at nine or ten o'clock, the buildings
Give off an unexpected heat; it has rained
This day, and the night before. I have spent them
At the movies, watching Bud Abbott and Lou Costello
Weary stark flat slapstick, but offering conditions
Questions, occasions for grieved analyses.
Do you not laugh, do you not cry?
What is real? cried the oyster, glob of spit
In a pane of glass.

# ALBANY PARK: CHICAGO

We are in Chicago's Waldheim cemetery.
I am walking with my father.
My nose, my eyes,
    left pink wrinkled oversize
        ear
My whole face is in my armpit.

We are at the stone beneath which lies
My father's mother;
There is embedded in it a pearl-shaped portrait.
I do not know this woman.
        I never saw her.
I am suddenly enraged, indignant.
I clench my fists; I would like to strike her.
My father weeps.
He is Russian; he weeps with
        conviction, sincerity, enthusiasm.
I am attentive.
I stand there listening beside him.
After a while, a little bored,
        but moved,
I decide myself to make the effort;
I have paid strict attention;
I have listened carefully.
Now, I too will attempt tears;
        they are like song.
        they are like flight.
I fail.

# NEW HAMPSHIRE: SEPTEMBER

The trees bend, the colors run —
Reds into yellow, greens,
                    grays
Into white.
        The bark, birch-bark,
Slips from its tree;
           September,
(Wet leaves, the sun falling still,
Compost,
        the hush of things burning,
   birdsong . . . )

                  pine trees
     white, white night light
Steaming, all cool in a mist.

# ATTIC BY THE RIVER

I walk by the used river
Each day
    past an old attic
(No house, the attic only
Beech trees growing through it)
In a field. The river smells
Of barges, rotting timbers
    waterskiers' boats, lovers
The very sun upon it.
Rivers age in Connecticut,
Grow feeble, irritable
And complain like old women.
The charred attic, too,
    complains
Bears ill-will toward people,
    weeps
And cries, and talks aloud
On certain evenings
    to the sea.

# THE CEILING

John liked ceilings;
he liked them very high
in the morning,
and then low at night.

At dawn he liked
a distance to rise to;
and in the evening
a closeness to sleep to.

John was indifferent
to floors, walls
          dazed even
in his walking
gazing, upon them.

In the afternoon he liked
a quiet ceiling, damp
and darkening
later, as the sky.

John passed from ceiling to ceiling;
and when it was very dark,
he'd turn on the light, open
the window and look at the night.

# A LETTER TO HIS PSYCHIATRIST

DEAR GEORGE — There was this sound. It was leaves.
It was outside the windows, outside
The house I live in, the house that is
Inside two other houses. And leaves.
It was just leaves. And the wind was leaves.
And there was the sound
                    . . . someplace in it
There was silence. Something that can kill you.
Worse than kill you. Make you into leaves.
Leaves in the leaves. Wind. Or the thing *fear*
Must always want, when there is nothing.
— I kept hearing it, the leaves against
Themselves. And the houses empty. Myself
And the sound. And my gun. — I went out,
Then, and shot the leaves. The trees. The wind.
I shot the wind, it was almost flesh,
It was leaves. It fell down on the lawn,
The uncut lawn. I shot it again.
And put it in my pocket. And walked
In the trees. And shot moths. And fireflies.
And my shadow, in the moonlight. Leaves . . .
                *        *        *
And then my wife was there, George. Calling.
Talking to me. Begging. But her voice —
It was not her at all. It was sound,
The sound of death in the sound of life.
Yet the voice, there was a voice. The leaves.
The night moths. It was *her* voice. Only,
As one must hear it, from the ghosts, the thing-ghosts
She felt she would become. Leaves. Of sound,
Of darkness, fire; of leaves, gnats and stones.

A voice like the single sound of death
Rapt, nun-toned, voiceless; and without sound . . .
Mindless. Incredible. Selfless. Fixed.
And she claimed she loved me. And loved me.
But as a ghost. As a *thing*. A thing
That must say, that must sound, all things
Alike, in the one way. And that must
Be heard as it is, by all the death
That is within one. That listens, speaks
Without surprise. And that is the ghost
That was one's flesh. Divorced into death.

## "... I HAVE JUST BOUGHT A HOUSE"

DEAR GEORGE — George, I have just bought a house,
An eighty-seven-room house. Also,
A twenty-one-room house. And many
Little houses. And eighteen trailers,
And nineteen cars (*six* with beds in them);
And wives for all the rooms, the trailers
The little houses, and the six cars
With beds in them,
          . . . and they all love me,
All my wives love me. They do, George. They
Write to me. Every day. They write
To me. And they are perfect, concise
And beautiful letters. They say —
Yes and they say it eighty-seven times.
And then sign their names. I taught them how,
                    George,
Myself. How to read and write. How to __
In houses. How to love, and how to
Write perfect, concise and beautiful
Letters. Yes, and how never to die;
How to live forever, for me, for
Me, even though *I* will die. And how
To make me feel as if I won't, even
Though I will, will feel as if I will.
And they are very good at it.
               Anyway,
They are all pregnant, George,
          all my wives
Are pregnant. Even the parakeets.
Because some of them are parakeets.
And some are goldfish,
          silverfish, ants

Rats, goats, skunks . . .
              and all have borne me children,
Parakeet, silverfish, ant, rat
                         goldfish
Children.
              And I'm happy, George. I like
Marriage, really like it; wives,
                         bedbugs
And getting mail every day.
And I feel I have a place to go.
It feels good.
                    The only trouble is
I don't have any money, or even
Any silverfish or rats or bedsheets
A newspaper, or a place to go.
I mean, why don't I, George?
                         I live alone
In an old upright typewriter,
                         with but
One dog and two cats to work
To cook, to drink beer with me.
It's sad, George. We cry ourselves
To sleep. We are so alone.
Now and then Dog sings to us —

        Woof, woof;
            pale cats, pale man
               you shall have houses,
               you shall have wives;
               *night falls*

        Woof, woof;
            beer for you, milk for you;
               sleep for you, dreams for you;

Sleep my children
sleep my children
sleep. Woof, woof.

It is a lovely song, George,
And Dog sings it well.
We sleep.

Witches,
Nightmares big as houses, wives
Warts, mushrooms,
they are all there is.
Night-things. Things —
pressing all the keys
Around us. Wanting what? To kill us;
To put us into jail.

Dog,
Dog barks, he barks songs at them.
They type *Death* onto his back,
Onto his tail, his ears, his tongue.
Fleas and lice!
We dance to avoid
The keys; we do not dance well.
We are typed into dreams, into wives;
Into mansions and swans;
old bedsheets, Death-sheets;
bedbugs
pushcarts and poems.

# ALL THE MORNINGS

All the mornings, always pennies
Of my life
Nickels, dimes
    shafts of light, clouds
Have begun
      over things — an alley,
Bushes, pawnshops,
        people.

It is a part of fish, rent-
  stench
Curtain smells,
      tenements
    to be three, four
Five flights above the street,
Over what in the good years
Of a good war one falls on
  now and then,
     dreams on, dies, a park.

All the evenings, always
      streetlights
Buildings, trees
   sculptured out of stone
       Moon
Nickels, dimes
  I'm falling,
    slowly
Quite slowly, now, down
Into the shafts of light.

# AN END TO DOUBT

After it was quiet,
the dust reflected
on the dust.

There was an end to doubt.

The stars were shown
    reflected
        in the stars,

            in the brackish, white, bleeding
                            triangles
        of light.

There was an end to doubt.

And all things,
    men and the moon,
        men and the remainders
                    of men,

        Cried out

And the stubbly,
now overgrown sea —

All, all things
    a part of the dust,
        not dead.

## PEOPLE GLOW

People glow. At certain times
They all come into themselves
And glow. It can be beheld.
It is a glorious thing;
To see it even
              is to glow.
And to speak of it well, that is
To cherish it, and glow.

Two still people in a still room.
It is of them that they have wings;
It is the thing of them that glows.
It is of us that we love
And dream, and are
              of stone.
I believe in stones, and am
And have ever been in love.

## FOR STONES

More and more one is aware in one's friends
Of an affection for stones.
Indeed, there are, of late, serious shortages,
A run on stones. And some persons, it is said,
Have formed "attachments" to them. By special decree,
Several have been executed.
Others are due soon to suffer that same fate.
Such measures are necessary. Who would deny it?
Things being what they are, the enemy
Approaching, the penalty foretold.
Surrender your stones. Lend us your support!

## STEEPLE

The clock.   Bonging away at midnight.
The moon a still, white, bent second hand,
          — at the peak of the spire.
The sky. The face of a black, stopped clock.

# THERE IS NO REASON WHY NOT
## TO LOOK AT DEATH

There is no reason why not to look at death.
A good poem, also, is also death-contained.
I once pulled out all the business feathers
Of a crow; he became better: godcomplete: black.

Nothing makes barely looking haste to put away
The dead: except the "dead" involved: in business.
The earth, the seasons, the poets, before they become
Poets, make no haste to put away the dead. Nor God

The Lord giveth, and He taketh away — by and large
Slowly. And without haste. Crow-bombs are here
Not my concern, nor ordinary bombs. But plain decay
(The proper autumnal process subsequent to life).

Emphasis need not be placed upon the soul. My point
Involves the leaf (as an example), and the unplumaged
Crow. Nor is my point one with flesh, and no blood . . .
But one of death. I am fond of death — and/or

The self-contained. This poem may not be said to be
About souls. But of things. Feathers and leaves.
Leafless trees and the featherless bodies of crows.
Finally, let us say, I have been asked to write simply.

# SCENES FROM A TEXT

> "Several *actual*, potentially and/or really
> traumatic situations are depicted on these pages."
>
> — *Transient Personality Reactions to Acute
> or Special Stress* (Chapter 5).

## PHOTO I

The car, a '39 Ford,
Lies on its side, windshield smashed
Doors off, bodies strewn, blood, brains
And tow-truck. A boy, perhaps
A girl, rushes about on fire,
And appears to have been so,
Now, for several moments. — Small,
Hairless, and with a face like
Sleep. In his bare, smoking arms
He carries a woman's head.
She is smiling, and her hair
Is all on fire. She too
Appears to be asleep. And the boy
Suddenly presses his head
                    down, *hard*
Into her neck,
            twists, and wears the head backwards.

## PHOTO II

The house is burning. The furniture
Is scattered on the lawn (tables, chairs
TV, refrigerator). Momma —
There is a small, superimposed white
Arrow pointing at her — is busy
Tearing out her eyes. The mute husband

(Named, arrowed) stands idly by, his hands
Upon his hips, eyes already out.
*The smoke blankets the sky.* And the scene,
Apart from Momma, Poppa, the flames . . .
Could be an auction. Friends, relatives
Neighbors, all stand by, reaching, fighting
For the mirrors, TV, sunglasses;
The children, the cats and speechless dogs.

## PHOTO III

The scene is an illuminated
Hole. Soldiers, firemen, are descending
(With axes, helmets) the nine ladders.
The moon watches over the shoulders
Of the crowd. Menninger, Murrow, wear earphones.
Unseen, asleep, awake, eighteen hundred feet
Down (where she has fallen, descended to
Willingly, confusing "up" and "down"),
With an NBC tape recorder,
— Instantly, specially lowered to her —
And companionable microphone,
The woman is rhythmically, for the
Moment, cursing, annihilating
Us all
          . . . the thick, dream-, lost, echoing voice
That one hears as one would hear one's own
(Oneself in a pit, cursing, pleading
Asleep, one's mind become as the earth,
Raging, damning, still, still, still, still, still,
An hysterical stone upon one)
— With indifference, interest, wonder
Or death
          . . . the scene stills, and is a photo.

## PHOTO IV

Three men in a canoe, in a flood;
Houses floating upsidedown, children,
Dogs, car-roofs, visible just beneath
The surface of the water. The men
Are dressed in raincoats, hats, faces, eyes:
All of which are composed of water.
*Shadows. Water. Black and white water.*
The sky, the floating, clapboard houses,
Are also composed of water. A scream!
The man's mouth is the sound of water;
The silence, swirling, the look of it.
It disappears, merges with his face.
And the leaden, still, almost churning
Wake, separate, identical with the flood,
Extends from the canoe back, ten,
Twenty, a thousand yards, to a house
Floating, still, in the distance. Shingled,
White, wooden water, a house of water.
(Like no, like all other houses, *death.*)
— A man, the one man with a paddle,
Begins drinking the scene, the water . . .
The other men, their raincoats, hats and eyes.
He becomes them, and the entire scene.
And all there is, is water, shadows
Water — or what might appear to be
Sleep, water, the inside of one's head.

# THE WEATHER

Black November    holy valley trees,
Spires,            churchstones
    Cowbells

           — It is

Evening.
    I am hanging, upside
Flaking, slowly
       the snow
    having watched, having watched
      THE WEATHER
            down.


# ALL FOR A DAY

All day I have written words;
My subject has been that. Words.
And I am wrong. And the words.
            I burn
Three pages of them. Words.
And the moon moonlight, that too
I burn. — A poem remains.
But in the words, in the *words*
In the fire that is now words.
I eat the words that remain,
And am eaten. By nothing,
By all that I have not made.

39

# FOR CHARLIE

It is after midnight. Another noon
And I'll be back in class, teaching midnight.
All the lunched-up faces. And me, a moon
Without a tie. They leave my class looking
For death. My examples are all myself.
The fluorescent lights are ghouls, I tell them.
Never smile beneath them. They eat teeth.
And last week I brought a body into class,
And nailed it to the blackboard — with three-inch
Lengths of chalk. Standing, then, in front of it,
I managed to murder their attention.
It was like the first time I called the roll:
And the dead all came to life. My zombies.
Without attention. — I put them to death.
Yes, you were right, Charlie: I'll never stand
Before them, and let them see themselves: taught,
By me.

# MY STUDENTS

It is them. I jump up and down hard
Very glad to see them. Jesus Christ.
They whistle, hoot, applaud, proud of me.
Then for hours, days, semesters, weeks
I do not say anything. It happens
Early in September. I break off
In the middle of something. And I stop.
I have nothing more to say to them.
They accept the fact. And are patient.
Meanwhile, I allow them to smoke.
At any time I may start in again. I sense
Their faith in me. And the Word is not yet,
Will not take hold, is not upon me.

# THE CYCLADES

"The Greek islands,
Mykonos,
Tinos, Siros,
yes, yes,"
said the blowfish,
conferring momentarily
with a stone,
with an octopus
and a whale,
"natural things
come from the world!"

\*      \*      \*

*They are composed, in the north,*
*of limestone, gneiss, schist and marble;*
*in the south, of eruptive rock, lava, basalt*
*and trachyte . . .*

ii

Lying awake
after billiards
(pocket billiards),
having lost,
having lost
I attempt again the "break";

I neither make,
nor see it made
(nor try)
but hear it,
clearly,
and lie entranced

42

as,
 moving, coming
   off the cushions,
     ceaselessly,
 uncontrollably,
       never dropping,
   the balls await,
       in motion
 some miracle of will.

   iii
 Pink cat,
  skin only
   in the white street,
     lizard bones
    twitching
     mule slop,
       church bells
 Mobil (and olive) oil
     cans, rusting;
       it lives,
        blinks,
        blind
         crawls
 (gnats and flies)
 umbrella frames
   licking like life
      the earth.

   iv
 Two old men, brothers
   the oldest in Piraeus,
     sailors
      part-time thieves,

43

smugglers,
and uncles to my wife,
appear
one upon the shoulders
of the other,
midnight
at a daughter's *Taverna*
drunk
O gloriously drunk
upon the family mule.

Introductions completed,
we observe the mule
(an enormous fish, perhaps
an elephant,
two other uncles
or a unicorn)
sipping beer.

v
Spidery-legged
in sunlight
on dusty duty rock,
sentry
the red ant
runs
sand grain
web-thread
*that* thin
knives
(the blades)
all around him.
The time:
9:30 A.M.

\*       \*       \*

I observe this on my way
  (squinting, bemused
mildly dysenteric),
        on a guided tour
    through Delos.

    vi
          *Statue*
Front view, tall
    very thin
    marble, white
        nude
      a sort of pillar
          stone-like
        only glowing,
    Woman
        rigid, arms
          straight
            and straight down;
  the Cycladic Mother Goddess
            One, stylized
          highbreasted
                  dimensional
    PERFECT!
  nose only, Big, wedge-shaped
      and those,
        her gigantic feet —
no eyes or mouth or hair.

    vii
"Chryssoula Koramidou, 45, yesterday
gave birth to twins in a Xanthi — Melissa bus
without being noticed by any of the
twenty passengers."
              — The Athens *News*, Saturday,
                  **August 5, 1961**

viii

Twelve years later,
    on a fig tree
        near Sounion,
    we observe
        (blooming),
three hundred and eighty-four
edible white baby bonnets;
        and the bruised,
    plum-colored fruit.

     *        *        *

        Black Greek goat
        ("time is memory"),
        six-inch
          eyelashes —
            blinking.

ix

Death this time in the uniform
    of an American naval officer,
        black armband
      sunglasses
          guidebook
      camera
           pilot's wings
and a live rose (white) in each hand;

Death in mourning for whom?
        for what? and why?

# BEFORE FIRING

. . . before firing
in
machine-gun practice,
we hesitated
for the butterfly
who came . . .

I fed a Browning-burst
of fifties
and he who squeezed
and I who fed
looked at sparkles
resting
in
the
silent air.

## DEDICATION

It is a jet-delight
for me, today
to stand
flown to you, friends,
over the body
of this . . .
a well-known soldier.

Firing a volley (FIRE!)
through the flag,
and into his death
we note
just how little
this boy
has passed beyond us.

*The body spurts, black*
*against the flag; and all*
*peer down*
*into its holes.* Notice
how little blood he sheds:
this is one of the finer restraints
of soldierhood.

It is for us to stand
and to applaud
over this well- (FIRE!)
vollied corpse

         — and now, plunging
our tongues
into the flag, let us delight
in his presence here today.

**48**

# LETTER TO HIS FIRST DOG

DEAR GEORGE — Seven of your years to one
Of ours. You were six, less than a year,
And I was five, when that Buick got you.
I threw snowballs at every one
I saw, that winter. They'd stop sometimes
And I'd run, screaming for you, I don't
Know why. It was twenty years ago.
My mother said you'd gone to heaven.
St. George.
        And you were a good saint, George.
Only you never answered when I
Wrote to you. Only prayers. You were good
About prayers. The other George we got,
And George the third, George the fourth (the cat)
And George the fifth. By then I'd married
And that was the end, I thought, of saints
And dogs, and praying to dogs, to get dogs.
But now I have to write you, George, again.

The thing is this, I'm in a madhouse.
Not like ours. The other kind, like where
We used to hunt for rabbits, where you
Made the spaniel pregnant, and ate snakes.
And I've been telling them about you.
And they said to write you. No one
Would say what, or how. Just "Write to him  . . ."
So how are you, George? I'm well, but sick.
It's snowing here today, black and white:
When it doesn't melt, it's white. It's hard
To tell what it's going to do, falling.
People bet on black, and white
                by flakes.

And when they've fallen, things fall on them.
What is God like? My nurse says he's green
Like she is, and that he's a dog. Is it
You, George? Is that why you're so good on prayers?

Does what the weather is make any
Difference to you? And why, George, why?
Or the times I've written you? George,
Who are you, George? Do I disappoint
You? Why do they want me to write you?
Are you them? or are you me? or God?
Do you mind about the other dogs?
I've asked. No one here seems to think so.
That you wouldn't have let me have them
Otherwise. I love you, George. You're good.
You don't say anything, even when
I'm not like I was before. I change.
I can't help it. And I think you've changed
Too. Though I have no way of knowing.
I can only guess. And eat snakes,

and pray.

## PHOTOS OF SOME POETS

The oblique, who look at you
The direct, who look away.
In all cases one senses
The eye at some right distance
To mind, to self — to nothing.
And it is this sense perhaps
(Along with some "flash" of fright)
That helps make the faces one,
One, in an anthology
Of faces. Moments, extremes
Occur rarely. At least for me.
And yet I have watched, have gazed
At all these faces, not drunk
Not sick, not dreaming, writing
Or even bored, and thought, thought
Them poems: and embarrassed
Turned to the faces, themselves.

## PET SHOP

The hundred dollar cats, the sixty
Dollar dogs; the lions, the tigers;
The six miniature, white, snake-eating
Fish; the snakes, the monkeys (with grins like
Gelded poodles); the parakeets; owls
Flamingos, pink pigeons and the small, headless
Proprietor, silky, creeping and jeweled.

## MISS ELDERLI DORA DES MOINES
## — ONE MARCH

She began to blow away, and put her soft
Kernel lace starch of a palm to her hat;
It was soon against a cloud, and she
Blew beyond the highest stalks, beyond it.

The wind was as if it were the sky, wanting
To get blue back about itself, up up
Up, and away . . . d'Iowaed she went, higher
Than the highest tassels ever reached.

How-dee'do? bowed God, as the harmonicas
Were polkachomp-reeded forth, together
With an old gee-tar (chaw! Oops!!),
In the sweetcorn-tune . . . softstrummed silk.

# TURNPIKE

It was a hole, a leveled, paved, black, white hole
A green hole, a blue hole, grass, sky, billboards, air
And we were in the hole — into the air, trees
Grass . . . into what were the trees, the sky, in us.
And we were in the air, the hole that went through
Itself.
      All around us there was what we were
Passing through, inside, inside, inside ourselves.
And the hole was humming, clear, laned, green and paved
With black stripes. And there was nothing, the minutes
Miles when you thought of them, when they made you them,
The Buick, the speed, the dead skunks at the skunk-
Crossing, the deer — *I pressed down on the horn,*
*My hand became a fist, became a sound, a hole*
*At the end of my wrist,* braked *and the thing was dead.*
        *        *        *        *

*So,* said Death, the deer, sitting there, between us,
With the great, white butterfly — and we were off,
Riding through air, through trees, through grass
              . . . and we were
In the hole, and over the hole, and the hole
Went on forever, into the trees, grass, the sky
That was there, within us, paved, black, white, a rock
A ghost, a Buick-thing, turnpike . . . a token.

# VOYAGE

The journey is forever inward,
Through marriages, past divorce suits
Diabetes, dentures, horny toenails.
Outside I see elm trees and think aloud
Of elm trees. To hell with poetry,
I have given up on it. Becalmed,
Preoccupied, I am moving inward.

# MOTHERS-IN-LAW

Married twice now, I've had two
Mothers-in-law. One visited us
And required, upon departure,
The services of three gentlemen
    with shoehorns
To get her back into her large black
Studebaker.

    The other, Momma-law the Present,
Is (with the exclusion neither
    of that other,
      my wives
    nor the fathers-in-law
      of either marriage),
   that Studebaker.

## NIGHTGOWN, WIFE'S GOWN

Where do people go when they go to sleep?
I envy them. I want to go there too.
I am outside of them, married to them.
Nightgown, wife's gown, women that you look at,
Beside them — I knock on their shoulder blades
Ask to be let in. It is forbidden.
But you're my wife, I say. There is no reply.
Arms around her, I caress her wings.


## THAT THAT ALL ENCLOSES

The darkness, night, that that all encloses
Air, who what where then is not the sun?
                              here
Jesus on his knees. Can that be right? No,
Reader, I enjoin you to forget this.
One does not come out where one intended.
Enters in. I am mistaken. Exits
                    babbling.

# ADVERTISEMENTS

## CLASSIFIED — PETS

For adoption. Regretfully offer dog.
Dog. Black, tan markings. One quarter cat.
Apartment-size, mature, spayed, a good watcher.
Barks (woof!). Healthy, vegetarian.


## *SATURDAY REVIEW* — CLASSIFIED; PERSONAL

MAKE MELLOW MUSIC!
MAKE MELLOW MUSIC!
Immediately . . .
With an exotic
Imported rosewood
Recorder. Perfect
Intonation. Not
A toy! Tuned to the
Spheres. Free telescope,
And attachments . . .
*See them twinkle!*
Audience, instruction
Guaranteed!
      Poetry
(Why not you . . . ?)
Aspires to the state
Of music, mellow
Rosewood. Listen! Mmm.
PANPIPES. BOX 139.

# "THE VERY AIR HE BREATHES"

She lies upon a tawny mat
of effluence — and leopard spots.

And he (*he's hers*
*and she knows it!*)

Can but barely be seen, crouched
and to the left of her.

One ear, an eyebrow, and a bit of cheek
are all that show of him.

The caption (again) suggests that it is fun
(*fabulous fun*) being female

*At a time like this!* And, indeed,
it looks like fun.

Her eyes are huge and subtly closed
as leopard spots; and her lips are spread.

She is, in fact, a deodored leopardess
about to take the male.

But again, the caption: *You are the very air*
*he breathes* (the male is hard upon her).

She appears to be undisturbed by this;
and with both shaved armpits bared, she arches

For him. One is inclined to think of her
as being altogether without fear; she smiles,

And takes the male. Neither deodorant,
nor effluence, could do more.

                        She smiles,
and she lies there, the very air
he breathed.

## SOCRATES AT THE SYMPOSIUM

Of Love, my friends (after such sophistry
And praise as yours), may one presume? Well, then,
Let me begin by begging Agathon:
Good sir, is not your love a love for me?
And *not* a love for those who disagree?
Yes, true! And what is it that Love, again,
Is the love of? Speak! It is the love again
Of "Socrates." Love, then, and the Good, are me.
Explain! Is Love the love of something, or
The love of nothing? Something! Very true.
And Love desires the thing it loves. Right.
Is it, then, really me whom you adore?
Or is it nothing? O Socrates, it's you!
Then I am Good, and I am yours. Agreed!

# EMU: A LECTURE FOR VOICES;
## FOR STEREO

Three-toed, one-headed, its wings the size
Of chicken-feet — and largest (next to
The ostrich) of all existing birds . . .
The emu stands, colossal, ratite
Six feet high

                its god enplumaged, dark
Hidden in the dismal, drooping, soft
Brown hair.

           *Its hips, hump, its bulge, perhaps*
*Of flightlessness, or sky — appear as speed;*
*The stunted cause, the befeathered, round*
*Sloping, still embodiment of speed.*

The emu runs, swoop-skims, a two-shanked
One-humped, egg-hatched camel: the bird most
Like a camel.

              Avoiding deserts
However, the emu inhabits
Open fields and forests where, keeping
In small companies, it feeds on fruit
(Of the emu tree), herbage and roots . . .
Now and then booming, with subsequent,
And peculiarly hurried efforts,
At breeding.

            Extinct, in Tasmania
On Kangaroo, King and Wing Islands,
The bird is found, and in small numbers,
In Southeastern Australia.

                  **IT BREEDS.**
Its nest, as if it had been rolled in
And humped (in reverse), is a shallow

Sandy, green-egg-filled pit, the eggs of which, all
Nine (to thirteen), are incubated
By the cock, an earnest, familial
Type of ostrich.

     The young, at birth, bear thin
Length-striped down, are wattleless, and walk;
Cursëd, crane-necked, blank, dull adult-eyed
*Baby, camel, ostrich-ducks* . . . in file
Swift, point-beaked,

       *mothered, three-toed, one-headed*
— an image, but for the stripes (and down),
Of itself, in age.

     Its booming note, god
And size, are at rest in it, in its
Conspicuous state of egglessness.
*It screams, booms, bounds*

       . . . BECOMES IMMENSE, FLIES
Extinct, shaggy, stripeless (in age)

       FLOATS
Its head in the camel clouds, the hump
The bulge, the sandlessness that is God.

60

# DODO

The dodo is two feet high, and laughs.
A parrot, swan-sized, pig-, scale-legged
Bird. Neither parrot, nor pig, nor swan.
Its beak is the beak of a parrot,
A bare-cheeked, wholly beaked and speechless
Parrot. A bird incapable of
Anything — but laughter. And silence:
A silence that is laughter, and fact,
And a denial of fact (and bird).
It is a sort of turkey, only
Not a turkey; not anything. — Not
Able to sing, not able to dance
Not able to fly, not able to . . .
Cook. The Dutch called it the "nauseous bird,"
*Walguögel,* "the uncookable."
Its existence (extinct as it is)
Is from the Portuguese: *Doudo,* "dumb,"
"Stupid," "silly." And the story of its
Having been eaten, in the genus
Of the solitaire (on Rodriguez
Island), by hogs, certain sailors and monkeys:
*Didus ineptus.* A bird that aided
Its own digestion, of seeds and leaves,
By swallowing large stones. It has been called,
Though with birds (extinct or otherwise)
Crosses are a lie, a cross between
A turkey and a pigeon. The first,
It is claimed, won out; and, having won,
Took flight from flight (its wings but tails, gray-
Yellow tufted white). And for reasons
As yet unknown.

61

Its beak is laughter
And shines, in indifference, and size.
It has the meaning, for some, of wings:
Wings that have become a face: embodied
In a beak . . . and half the dodo's head . . .
*It laughs — silence, its mind, extends from its ears;*
*Its laugh, from wings, like wrists, to bill, to ears.*


## SNOW

The snow began to fall and, pleased
With its falling, and the thick
Light effect of itself, blackwhite
Against the summer, frozen
Town, it gathered in momentum
Independent of the wind
And let itself tumble, with a
Quick, sensual uncontrol . . .

Like some unmiraculous *white*
Of a woman, stripped and gathered
Into the lightest freezings
Of herself
                    — pleased by her being
And the thick of herself, as such,
Upon the dead spread of streets, steeples
And the noon hour of the night.

# THE IMMORTALS, IN QUESTION

"We are about to overtake our gods."

What will the gods do? There is
No place to hide. And how are
We to bear them? After all
The photographs are taken,
All the images recast
(Into rather more useful forms),
The ancient saints, priests, choir-
Boys (and girls) destroyed (organs,
The formerly holy stars,
The musical spheres . . . ),
Who will care for them, cleanse them,
Feed them?
　　　　　*What will the gods do?*

## BARBECUE

### — For W.D.

I

They were spraying 7-up and moth-juice
On the fire. The mosquitoes, lawn-flies
And moths dove, flashed and were painlessly
Consumed. There was applause
                              . . . we entered.
And while my wife was kissed, they clapped
Me on the back. They wanted to know
That I was there; and then I kissed them
Down their throats, choked and knew that they were there.

And after I had kissed those who had
Kissed my wife, and after they kissed me,
We sprayed one another, scratched and dove
After the moths. We flashed, painlessly,
And emerged to munch the ashes, coals
To sip moth-juice, 7-up and gin.
*And (again) we clapped one another*
*Laughed, kissed, sipped, puffed and swallowed cigarettes.*

II

When the Ginns arrived, they were pounded
On their backs. Our fists came out their mouths
(We all took turns laughing hands that way,
And toasting with one another.)
                              **Poor**
Wrist-throated Mrs. G.! She was mad.
Her breasts were ferocious olives. She
Wouldn't smile, or sip — and we all
Took turns mixing drinks through her (and Mr. G.)

**64**

## III

The cat-girl would not believe in it
And crouched there pained, purring with the pups;
(Their tails were remarkably alike
And neither pronounced upon events
With them.) From time to time they'd lick one
Another, or the cream-dip, but otherwise
Were still
          . . . though one of the pups had tried
The fire, and the cat-girl
          sleekly swallowed gin.

## IV

Someone found Lil, the wife of no one,
Buried beside the spit. She wanted
A martini; we obliged, and then
Reburied her.
          Fran nibbled at the
Charcoal in Bernie's fingernails.
               They'd
Expelled her from Home Economics.


And Bernie dove in after the moths
Only to be buried, topped, beside the spit.

## V

The sky was rainbow strips of chrome, clouds
And the sun, the great, archetypal
Ford: pork-sauced and on the suburban
Spit of heaven.
          And Lil's angel waved
Free, fulfilled and married now, to chrome
. . . sipping gin and tonic.

We all stared,
Climbed upon our spit, and then dove
In after the moths.
        — The fire attained to Lil.

Unfortunately, the rest of us
Did not. And we had to try to tell
(Again) whether or not we were there.
*The fire was a Ford, without chrome, pure*
*As gin, as cream-dip, moths or spray, death*
And we sang to it: its attaining
To heaven, to Lil, to space, ourselves
And the archetypal Ford.
        The Ford honked, then

Backed off its spit, and began to set.
In the other distance, in the space
The consuming that is east, the night
Beyond where the moths take form, beyond
What we flash for when we die,
        we sense
The white-walled dawn, time and tomorrow's
Ford.
      The cat-girl vomited, and there was Mars,
The suburban star of barbecue.

VI

The party had somehow failed. The cards —
And there was Rummy, large as Lil, four'd
The evening star. It was time for gin
And time for light!
        No one would admit
That he was there; we hid in front of
One another's wife. The women hid

Beside the flames — the way they flickered
Through their eyes. I kept trying to put my tongue

Into their cards, into their eyes, ears
Throats, between their teeth; but theirs were there
Between mine. I bit them. And they cried
With half their tongues
                                    munching diamonds and spades.

And the bushes had begun the moon,
Ending "gin," martinis and marriage.
Suddenly the women screamed. The moon
Burst through, revealing their husbands, the pup-girl

Themselves. The bushes became the lawn;
The night, the earth; and the moths, the sun.

The men became their wives; and the wives
Became the men, for the most part re-

Marrying themselves. The men were asleep
Beside their wives, smiling, spitted, still

Illicit. — Morning. My wife and I
Sipped gin; I was Bernie, and she the moths.